D0645725

Tail of the Moon

7

Story & Art by
Rinko Ueda

Tail of the Moon

Volume 7

CONTENTS

Chapter 43 4

Chapter 44 33

Chapter 45 59

Chapter 46 85

Chapter 47 113

Chapter 48 139

Chapter 49 165

Glossary 190

Story Thus Far...

It is the Era of the Warring States. Usagi is a failure as a ninja, but she is a skilled herbalist. She is working hard to qualify as a ninja so she can be the bride of Hattori Hanzo (aka "Shimo no Hanzo")!

Usagi is captured by Hikaru and taken to Kouga. Goemon comes to save her, but Hikaru forces him to drink an asphyxiation potion and attacks him! On top of being in bad shape because of the potion, Goemon is now critically wounded.

Later, Hikaru sets fire to the village and attacks village leader Kanbutsu, creating havoc everywhere. Surprisingly, Goemon tries to protect Hikaru. As it turns out, Goemon was once Hikaru's only childhood friend. Because Goemon unintentionally broke a promise he made to Hikaru, Hikaru has not been able to believe in anyone since then...

The incident at Kouga was settled, and Usagi returns to Iga to practice her ninjutsu. Suddenly, her great-grandfather appears and tells Hanzo the engagement is cancelled?!

"CONSIDER THIS ENGAGEMENT CANCELLED."
GREAT-GRANDPA?!

Chapter 43
Tail of the Moon™

TAIL OF THE MOON EXTRA: TODAY'S MISSION

"I WANT TO SEE USAGI DO SYNCHRONIZED SWIMMING."

-TANII, SAITAMA PREFECTURE

SHRIEK
I'M SAYING IT FOR YOUR SAKE, USAGI...
WHY ARE YOU SAYING THAT ALL OF A SUDDEN?!
SHRIEK
VERY WELL.

HANZO?!
THIS WAS AN UNWANTED ENGAGEMENT FOR ME FROM THE START...
...SO I'M RELIEVED TO HEAR THAT.
HMM...
THEN WE HAVE...AN AGREEMENT.

UNWANTED
WAS I NOTHING MORE THAN AN UNWANTED PERSON...
...TO HANZO?
USAGI.
COLLECT YOUR BELONGINGS. WE'RE GOING BACK TO HOJIRO.

IT WOULD HAVE HAPPENED SOONER OR LATER...
CANCELLED ?!

I CAN'T DO ANYTHING...
GOEMON, DON'T GET TOO EXCITED...
USAGI...
AND YOU'RE OKAY WITH THAT ?!

HANZO SAID IT WAS AN UNWANTED ENGAGEMENT...

I WAS EXPECTING EITHER...
"I WILL NOT CANCEL THE ENGAGEMENT!!" OR...
"USAGI IS THE ONLY PERSON FOR ME!!"
You sound so much like him...
I NEVER THOUGHT HANZO WOULD ACTUALLY AGREE...
WHOA!
MASTER!!
I WAS SO SURE THAT HE WOULD SAY THAT...
SO YOU WERE TRYING TO TRICK HANZO, MASTER?
YOU'RE SUCH A MEAN OLD MAN!!
BUT...
AT LEAST I KNOW HOW HANZO REALLY FEELS NOW, SO...
HE DIDN'T MEAN IT!!
WAK
HANZOU...
DON'T CANCEL THE ENGAGEMENT, USAGI!!

IT WAS JUST A TIT FOR TAT RESPONSE ON HANZO'S PART.
HE'S NEVER BEEN GOOD AT SAYING HOW HE REALLY FEELS...
JUST FORGET IT.
I DON'T WANT HANZO TO DISLIKE ME EVEN MORE!!
USAGI...
GREAT-GRANDPA...
I'M READY TO GO HOME!!

GREETINGS
Hello! Ue-Rin here.
I'm going to continue the "Ue-Rin's Manga School" from the last volume.
RIN
Last time, we ended with Ue-Rin sending in her manga for the first time...
...and the result was...
IT DOESN'T HELP YOU LOSE WEIGHT, BUT IT DOES HELP YOU FEEL REFRESHED. ENJOY IT WITH THE OTHERS.
OH, HANZOU...
...YOU CAN HAVE THE TEA I MADE.
OOF
HEY USAGI, YOU SHOULD HELP WITH CARRYING GOEMON, TOO.
TMP
OOF
BYE!!
Sorry, Master...
TMP

ZWAK
TMP
TMP
HANZO!
IF YOU'RE GOING TO GO AFTER HER, NOW'S THE TIME TO DO IT!
BUT THAT CAN WAIT, CAN'T IT?!
I'M WORKING RIGHT NOW.
HURRY UP AND GO AFTER HER!!
BUT I'M FINALLY BACK TO AN ENVIRONMENT WHERE I CAN WORK IN SILENCE.
THEN WHY DON'T YOU MARRY YOUR JOB!!
...
ZWAK!

TP
STOP...
...CLOUDING MY MIND...
DON'T YOU NEED TO GO HOME, YURI?
NOPE!
I'M GOING TO TAKE CARE OF GOEMON.
USA...
YOU'RE NOT MARRYING HANZO ANYMORE?
YEAH ...

I'M SORRY, USA...
USAGI...
ONCE YOU'RE BACK AT THE VILLAGE, YOU CAN EAT SOME DELICIOUS FOOD AND CHEER UP.
HANZO'S HOUSE...
A PLACE WHERE I EXPERIENCED MUCH HAPPINESS AND SADNESS...
I WISH I HAD BEEN ABLE TO SEE...
...HANZO'S FACE AGAIN FOR ONE LAST TIME...

USAGI...
WELCOME HOME.
HOJIRO
WHAT A RUDE GIRL...
HE'S MY SON, SANDAYU.
YOU'RE A TWIN, OLD MAN?!
WHOA!
HI, GRANDPA...
TMP TMP TMP TMP
FOREVER?
FOREVER...
HOW LONG ARE YOU GOING TO BE HERE THIS TIME?
USAGI...

HUH?!
YAY!
WELCOME BACK! ♡
GOEMON...
HEEEEY...
NO, I'LL...
I'LL LOOK AFTER YOU.
OHH...
YOU LOOK JUST AWFUL, GOEMON!!
GOEMON'S MINE...!!
Usagi...
SHOVE
Oww
USA...I'M STARVING...
WHOA!
LET'S COOK SOMETHING, SHALL WE?
BICKER BICKER

IF THIS WAS HANZO'S KITCHEN, I'D KNOW WHERE EVERYTHING WAS...
Not here either.
COME TO THINK OF IT... I WAS BORN HERE, BUT I'VE NEVER USED THIS KITCHEN BEFORE...
WHERE'S THE RICE?
UM...

I FOUND THE RICE.
USA...

USA...?
TMP TMP

SNIFF...
"DON'T ASSUME TO KNOW YOUR OWN LIMITS!!"
HANZO...
"YOU ARE GOING TO BE QUALIFIED AS A NINJA AND BECOME MY WIFE."
MY HOME IS WHERE HANZO IS.
"HOME IS WHERE I AM, USAGI."

BUT I CAN'T GO BACK ANYMORE...

WHAT...?
WHO MADE ALL THIS DELICIOUS-LOOKING FOOD?!
USA DID.
IS THAT TRUE?!
MAMEZO...
I'LL HAVE THE WHOLE BUCKET.
LET'S EAT...
Let's eat!!
USAGI'S EATING THE WHOLE POT...
WELL, SHE IS A GROWING CHILD...
I'VE GOT NO REASON TO BE ON A DIET ANYMORE.
YOU'VE GOT NO REASON TO BE GAINING WEIGHT EITHER...
DELICIOUS!
USAGI, YOU'RE A MASTER COOK!!

IF YOU MARRY GOEMON, YOU'LL ALWAYS BE WITH US.
WELL, YOU CAN ALWAYS MARRY GOEMON.
DON'T BE SO SELFISH, YOU TWO!!
BUT I COULDN'T GET MARRIED!!
NOW YOU CAN GET MARRIED ANYTIME...
I'm so relieved!

I'M NOT HUNGRY...
SIGH...

GOEMON, I'VE BROUGHT YOU SOME FOOD...
SHIK

I CAN'T BELIEVE USA LEFT HER FOOD...
I'LL GO TAKE SOME FOOD DOWN TO GOEMON.

THOK
WHA...
WHAT ARE YOU DOING?!
WE'RE FIGHTING TO SEE WHO'S GOING TO CHANGE GOEMON'S BANDAGES!!
I'M NOT GOING TO LET SOME NEWCOMER DO IT!!
Hey...
Stop it...
HOW DARE YOU SAY THAT TO ME?
THERE'S NO NEED TO FIGHT...
It's dangerous, you guys...
NO NEED TO FIGHT?!

IT'S YOUR FAULT GOEMON'S WOUNDED IN THE FIRST PLACE, ISN'T IT?!
UH...
YOU'RE THE CAUSE AGAIN, USAGI?!
WE'VE REALLY HAD ENOUGH...
I...I'M SORRY...
WE DON'T WANT YOU TO HAVE ANYTHING TO DO WITH GOEMON FROM NOW ON.
STOP IT!!
I'M RESPONSIBLE FOR THESE WOUNDS.
USAGI HAD NOTHING TO DO WITH IT!

BUT...
GET OUT.
I'LL HAVE USAGI CHANGE THE BANDAGES.
YOUR FOOD'S READY, SO WHY DON'T YOU GO EAT?
WHAT ABOUT ME...?
DEJECTED
OH... OKAY...
I'LL change the bandages first.
I WON'T TOLERATE ANYONE BEING MEAN TO YOU!
GOEMON...
YOU DIDN'T HAVE TO BE SO HARSH WITH THEM...
FINE, BUT I GET TO CHANGE THE BANDAGES NEXT...
TMP
TMP

THEY'RE NOT BEING MEAN TO ME.
HUH...
THEN WHY DO YOU LOOK LIKE YOU'RE ABOUT TO CRY?
DO I?
GRAB
FOR GOD'S SAKE...
GOEMON...

WHA...
SNORT
'CAUSE YOU'RE CRYING.
WHAT WAS THAT FOR?!
DOOK
WAAAAARGH
WHAT'S WRONG WITH ME CRYING...!!
THERE'S NOTHING WRONG WITH IT.
YOU'VE DONE NOTHING WRONG, USAGI.
There, there.
HANZO'S...

WAARGH...
YOU'LL FEEL A LOT BETTER ONCE YOU CRY IT ALL OUT.
WAARGH...
THE RAIN'S BOUND TO STOP, RIGHT?

LOOK AT ME.
I'M YOUR SUN, USAGI.

YOU JUST NEED TO BE LOOKING AT ME...

TAIL OF THE MOON EXTRA: TODAY'S MISSION

"I WANT TO SEE HANZO IN 'WINTER SONATA.'♡"

–SUZUZOU, FUKUSHIMA PREFECTURE

YURI, YOU LOOK SO CUTE! ♡
HANZO'S TRIVIA
IN GERMAN, A HANG-OVER IS DESCRIBED AS "HAVING A MALE CAT."
Tail of the Moon
Chapter 44

YOU JUST NEED TO BE LOOKING AT ME...
STOP IT!!
THUNK
URGH

I'M...
...GOING TO SHAVE MY HEAD BALD AND BECOME A NUN!!
HUH?
Hey, you've got a cut on your forehead.
OWWW
I'M GOING TO LIVE ALL ALONE AND HOLD A SERVICE FOR MY FEELINGS FOR HANZO!
WHAT ARE YOU TALKING ABOUT?
NANMAIDA...
NANMAIDA...
OW...
OWW...

I can do some needle-work, too.
I LEARNED HOW TO COOK AND CLEAN...
BUT...
IF YOU'VE GOT THE GUTS TO SHAVE YOUR HEAD, WHY DON'T YOU WORK HARD AT TRYING TO MAKE HANZO PAY ATTENTION TO YOU?
I DID TRY HARD!!
I'M IN LOVE WITH HANZO...
HE'S THE ONLY ONE I CAN THINK OF!!
OH FOR CRYIN'...
BUT HANZO...
...DECIDED TO BREAK OFF THE ENGAGEMENT...
BUT WHAT?

HANZO'S PERFECT.
MAYBE I'M JUST NOT GOOD ENOUGH FOR HIM...
HANZO'S PERFECT?!
COME ON, NOBODY'S PERFECT.
WELL, HANZO IS PERFECT!!
GOEMON...
WHAT IS IT THAT I LACK?!
YOU'RE FINE THE WAY YOU ARE, USAGI.
BUT THAT WON'T DO...!!
THEN THINK ABOUT IT BY YOURSELF!!
I'm going to sleep.
UP

SHOCK
WHAT YOU LACK?
WELL, THERE'S A TON OF THINGS YOU LACK...
...BUT THE THINGS YOU LACK THE MOST ARE BEAUTY AND SEX APPEAL.
GIRLS CAN ALWAYS MAKE THEMSELVES LOOK MORE BEAUTIFUL.
YOU REALLY ARE STUPID.
SOB
SOB
BUT I'LL NEVER BE ABLE TO DO ANYTHING ABOUT THAT...

UE-RIN'S WAY OF THE MANGA 6

The reality hit Ue-Rin right in the face... Ue-Rin was forced to realize her lack of skills...

I wasn't sad, but I was frustrated.

However, the "Manga School" I sent my work to was a special edition where a brief comment and an image from the work of all the people who applied were printed in the magazine. So even though my work was rejected, I was really happy to see a small image of it in print.

SWIP
HEY!
YURI'S PUTTING MAKE-UP ON ME.
!!

TMP
TMP
I... I'M SO GLAD...
USA, WHAT ARE YOU DOING?
STOP CRYING. IT'S GOING TO BE HARDER FOR ME TO PUT MAKE-UP ON YOUR FACE IF YOU CRY.

UP
HUH?
WAAAARGH
USA'S TURNED INTO A MONSTER...!!

THAT'S BECAUSE YOU STARTED CRYING WITH THAT AWFUL FACE OF YOURS...!!
I LOOK WORSE THAN BEFORE!!
BICKER
BICKER

BOING
!!

HOP
MAYBE THE EASIEST WAY TO GET TO HANZO IS TO PRACTICE EVERY DAY AND BECOME QUALIFIED...
You can do it, Usa...
SIGH...
THE NEXT DAY
TMP TMP TMP
"IT'S YOUR TREE, USAGI."
YIKES
GRACK
HE'S GOING TO HATE ME EVEN MORE AFTER SEEING IT...
HOP
HANZO'S PROBABLY NOTICED IT BY NOW...
THE BROKEN SEEDLING...

TUP
SWIFTLY...
MOVE SWIFTLY...
TROMP
TROMP
MASTER HANZO...
I SEE THAT EVERYONE'S WORKING HARD.
WE NEVER KNOW WHEN ODA'S ARMY WILL STRIKE NEXT.
I'LL HAVE THEM START ATTENDING FIELD EXERCISES, TOO.
GOOD.
SOUNDS FINE.
I THINK THE SENIOR STUDENTS ARE READY TO BE QUALIFIED.

TROMP
TROMP
"NOOO, DON'T TELL HIM, GREAT-GRANDPA...!!"
SO THIS IS WHAT SHE WAS TALKING ABOUT...

ARE YOU SERIOUS?!
HANZOU...?
DON'T RAISE YOUR VOICE.
BUT THINK ABOUT IT...
WE CAN'T JUST TAKE USAGI WITH US.
AND IT'S A SECRET THAT YOU'RE EVEN LIVING IN IGA...
SPRING
WHAT'S WRONG?
SHUSH
SOMEONE'S OVER THERE.
I DON'T SEE ANYBODY.
BUT I FELT SOMEONE'S PRESENCE...
I KNOW.
WHY DON'T WE GET SOMEBODY TO TAKE HER PLACE?!
HE'D NEVER FALL FOR THAT.

MAYBE I'LL ASK HANZO ABOUT IT.
ISN'T IT OBVIOUS THAT HE'D OBJECT?!
I'LL DO SOMETHING ABOUT IT...
I'LL GO WITH YOU...
NO...
YOU'RE PREGNANT, SARA.
YOU HAVE TO STAY INSIDE WHERE IT'S SAFE!!
HANZOU...
DON'T WORRY.
I'LL MANAGE SOMEHOW.

THIS TEA HAS SUCH A LOVELY ROASTED SCENT.
SO THIS IS THE TEA USAGI MADE...
SHE ORIGINALLY WANTED TO MAKE A WEIGHT-LOSS TEA BUT ENDED UP WITH THIS INSTEAD.
IT TASTES GOOD ENOUGH TO BE SOLD AT A SHOP THOUGH...
I SHOULD HAVE ASKED HER HOW SHE MADE IT.
A BATH, HUH?
WOULD YOU LIKE TO HAVE SOME OF USAGI'S TEA?
HEY...
IS HANZO AROUND?
MASTER HANZO'S GONE TO TAKE A BATH.
I'M A LITTLE BUSY RIGHT NOW...
TELL HANZO I'M GOING BACK TO HAMAMATSU AND WON'T BE BACK FOR A WHILE.

AREN'T YOU GOING TO PRACTICE YOUR JUMPS TODAY...?
USA...
MY SPRAINED ANKLE IS BEGINNING TO HURT AGAIN, SO I'M GOING TO REST UP...
DID YOU RUB SOME OINTMENT ON IT?
SLUGGISH
I DID.
MAMEZO, CAN YOU GIVE ME A MASSAGE?
AND MY NECK'S REALLY STIFF, TOO...
OKAY!
HARDER, MAMEZO.
MPH
MPH
GRP
GRP
OOOH...
THAT'S IT... ♡
KNEAD
I NEVER KNEW YOU COULD SOUND SO SEXY.

YOU CAUGHT ME BY SUR-PRISE.
I NEVER THOUGHT YOU'D DROP BY MY PLACE.
TMP
TMP
I KNOW.
HERE'S SOME TEA.
HIYA!
HANZOU ?!
YOUR TEA'S BECOME QUITE A HIT, USAGI.
THANKS!
HAS HANZO TRIED IT, TOO?!
NO...
HE ONLY DRINKS HOT WATER.

THERE'S A MAN WHO'S TAKEN A GREAT LIKING TO YOUR TEA, USAGI...
OH...
SPROING
IS IT HANZO?!
NO.
SHOVE
TCH!
AS A MATTER OF FACT...
...THERE'S SOMEBODY WHO'D LIKE TO SEE YOU, USAGI...
...AND YOU MAY BE SURPRISED TO HEAR WHO IT IS, BUT...
MAMEZO...
NO, NOT THERE!
GRRP
GRRP
HIGHER, MAMEZO.
LISTEN TO ME!!
I AM LISTENING...
SARA'S FATHER WANTS TO SEE YOU.
THE PRINCESS'S FATHER IS...
Oooh, that's it...
...LORD ODA NOBUNAGA.

HUH...
SARA SENT SOME OF YOUR TEA DOWN TO AZUCHI, AND LORD NOBUNAGA LIKED IT A LOT.
HE WANTS TO MEET THE PERSON WHO MADE IT.
ODA NOBUNAGA WANTS TO SEE ME?!
WHAAAAAAT
WHOA

WHO'S THAT?
A...A REALLY SCARY LORD WHO HATES NINJA!!
HE'S OUR ENEMY!!
ENEMY, I SAY!
YOU CAN HIDE YOUR IDENTITY AND MEET HIM...
NO WAY!!
NEVER!
I DON'T WANT TO DIE YET!!
I'LL GO WITH YOU.
NOOO...
GO...
...USAGI.
GREAT-GRANDPA ?!
GET CLOSE TO NOBUNAGA...
...AND FIND OUT WHAT THE SITUATION IS IN AZUCHI.

I CAN'T DO THAT!!
IF YOU CAN SUCCESSFULLY ACCOMPLISH THIS BIG TASK...
...I'M WILLING TO GIVE YOU YOUR QUALIFICATION.
QUALIFICATION...?
TH... THAT'S RIGHT!!
I BET HANZO WOULD BE REALLY IMPRESSED IF HE FOUND OUT YOU QUALIFIED AS A NINJA!!
HANZO...
...WILL BE IMPRESSED WITH ME...
MULL

OKAY!
I'LL GO SEE NOBUNAGA AND GET MY QUALIFICATION!!
YOU DON'T HAVE TO SAY ANYTHING, USAGI.
JUST LEAVE EVERY-THING TO ME.
OHHH
JUST YOU WAIT AND SEE, NOBU-NAGA...
WELL SAID!!
IT'S NOT NOBUNAGA, BUT "LORD NOBUNAGA," OKAY?!
I CAN'T LET YOU DO THIS, HANZOU.

I'LL ACCOMPANY HER TO AZUCHI.
HANZO?!
HAN...
...ZO...?

HANZO, WHEN DID YOU...
I CAN SEE RIGHT THROUGH EVERYTHING YOU DO, HANZOU.
YOU'RE COMING WITH ME...?
THIS IS THE PERFECT OPPORTUNITY TO FIND OUT NOBUNAGA'S TRUE INTENTIONS OF ATTACKING IGA.
I'LL GO TOO...
JUST USAGI AND I WILL BE FINE.
TUG
OH...

USAGI AND I WILL ENTER AZUCHI POSING AS A HUSBAND AND WIFE RUNNING A TEA PLANTATION.

AS HUSBAND AND WIFE...
...WITH HANZO?!

TAIL OF THE MOON EXTRA: TODAY'S MISSION

"I WANT TO SEE HANZO IN A LITTLE LEAGUE LOOK." ♡

-KYAKYA, SAITAMA PREFECTURE

Tail of the Moon
Chapter 45
HANZO'S TRIVIA
WHEN CLEANING AN EEL, THE EEL IS CUT FROM THE BACK IN THE KANTO REGION AND FROM THE STOMACH IN THE KANSAI REGION.

"USAGI AND I WILL ENTER AZUCHI POSING AS A HUSBAND AND WIFE RUNNING A TEA PLANTATION."

IF HE'S ACCOMPANYING YOU, THEN THERE'S NOTHING TO WORRY ABOUT, USAGI!!
THAT'S GREAT!!
UM...
...CHANGE INTO THIS.
USAGI...
SWUP
GREAT-GRANDPA...
YOU LOOK THE OTHER WAY, HANZOU.
I'LL UNDRESS YOU. ♪
HURRY UP AND GET CHANGED.
"GOOD DEEDS SHOULD BE DONE WITHOUT HESITATION."
HUH?!
WAAAARGH
WHAT'S WRONG, USA...?!
TMP
TMP
AAAAAAH!

MAMEZO...
USAGI AND I WILL BE AWAY FOR A WHILE.
MA... MAMEZO...
YOU LOOK SO PRETTY, USA! ♪
TAKE THIS WITH YOU.
CINCH
FAMILY HISTORY?!
SWIP
BEFORE WE LEAVE, MAKE SURE YOU KNOW THE FAMILY HISTORY OF THE COUPLE WE'RE GOING TO BE PORTRAYING.
USAGI...
...JUST AROUND THE CORNER...
JU...
GASP...
GASP...
WHERE ARE YOU GOING, USA?

...PRETEND TO BE HANZO'S WIFE...
You started off with how the two met each other?!
Of course.
I CAN'T...
I'LL ASSUME THE NAME OF "HANBEI." USAGI, YOU'LL BE "KAYO."
HANZO, WHEN DID YOU MAKE THIS?
WE'LL START CALLING EACH OTHER BY THOSE NAMES FROM NOW ON.
YOU SURE ARE A HARD WORKER...
WE JUST BROKE OFF OUR ENGAGE-MENT...
...THAT'S HOW IT GOES.
DID YOU GET THAT, "KAYO"...?

THAT'S YOUR NAME.
YOU'RE TO RESPOND AT ONCE!!
I THINK IT'S A LITTLE TOO HARD FOR USAGI.
WHY DON'T YOU JUST CALL HER USAGI?
MY NAME?!
B-BUMP B-BUMP
JOLT
KAYO!!
WHOA
THEN...I'LL CALL YOU BY YOUR NAME, USAGI.
BUT YOU MUST CALL ME "HANBEI."
GIVE IT A TRY.
USAGI!!
ZWAK
HANZO...
OK...
TAKE THE "MASTER" OFF!!
BUMP
M...MASTER HANBEI?
BUMP
GOEMON?!
I HEARD YOU'RE GOING TO AZUCHI...
IS THAT TRUE?!

I'LL ACCOMPANY HER TO AZUCHI.
GOEMON...
YOU SHOULDN'T MOVE YET!!
IT'S TOO DANGEROUS TO TAKE USAGI TO AZUCHI!!
DAMN YOU...
YOU ALWAYS APPEAR WHEN THINGS ARE CONVENIENT FOR YOU...
IT'S OKAY...
...GOEMON.

SO...
IF I SUCCEED, I'M GOING TO BE QUALIFIED AS A NINJA!!
ALL RIGHT...
...TAKE CARE OF USAGI FOR ME.
HANZO...

I WILL.
LET'S GO.
HANZO!!
YE... YES...
I'M WORRIED.
NO, THAT'S WRONG!!
I'M SORRY, HANZO...
IT'S HANBEI!!

I WAS READY TO GO TO AZUCHI...
...BUT I NEVER THOUGHT I'D BE GOING THERE WITH HANZO...
HUFF
HUFF
AND ON TOP OF THAT...
...AS HUSBAND AND WIFE...
USAGI...
I WON'T RESPOND TO YOU UNLESS YOU START CALLING ME "HANBEI" FROM NOW ON.
!!
WHEEZE
WHEEZE
WHY ARE YOU WALKING SO SLOWLY?!
M... MY LEG HURTS...
THE SEEDLING...
I SPRAINED MY FOOT... WHEN I WAS PRACTICING... JUMPING OVER IT...
PANT... PANT...
SHA

IT'LL BE TOUGH FOR YOU TO CROSS THE MOUNTAINS WITH THAT LEG OF YOURS.
GET ON MY BACK.
LIKE HUSBAND AND WIFE...

HOLD ON TIGHTER.
O... OKAY.
CLUTCH
I HAVE TO ACT LIKE HIS WIFE...
SO, FOR THE DURATION OF THIS TRIP...

...MAYBE HE'LL BE KINDER TO ME...
WE'LL DROP BY UJI BEFORE GOING TO AZUCHI.
UJI?!
WE'RE GOING TO VISIT A REAL TEA PLANTATION IN UJI.
WE...WE HAVE TO DO THAT?!
OF COURSE.
I HEAR THAT NOBUNAGA KNOWS A LOT ABOUT TEA...
...SO WE MUST BE READY TO ANSWER ANY QUESTIONS HE ASKS US ABOUT IT.
RIGHT...

COLORED RICE?
?
USAGI...
THIS IS JUST AN ASSIGNMENT.
...GET OFF MY BACK HERE.
IT'S CALLED FIVE-COLORED RICE...
...AND VARIOUS COMBINATIONS OF THESE COLORS MAKE UP SECRET CODES.
PEOPLE USED TO SCOLD ME WHEN I WAS SMALL SINCE I ATE THEM ALL THE TIME...
OF COURSE YOU'D BE SCOLDED.
THE RICE WAS DYED SO THAT BIRDS AND INSECTS WON'T EAT THEM IN THE FIRST PLACE...
USAGI...
I WANT YOU TO PRAY TO THIS JIZO STATUE.
HUH?
OKAY...
NAMU... NAMU...
I'M DONE.
NOT YET.

UE-RIN'S WAY OF THE MANGA ⑦

"Making my debut with the first manga I sent" ♪

Not only did that dream not come true, but I was faced with a huge sense of loss as well. I decided to take a good look at the reason behind my failure.

My current self + What I lack = Final result

Though I was one of the better drawers at school, there were a lot of people who were far better than me out in the world. Even if I work ten times as hard as those people, I may never be able to get half as good as them...But I'll do what I can!!

Come to think of it, I was a pretty passionate middle schooler...

I DIDN'T GIVE YOU ANY ORDERS TO GO OUTSIDE ON AN ASSIGNMENT.
WE'RE ON OUR WAY TO OUR ASSIGNMENT AS WELL...
B-BUMP
B-BUMP

MA...
...MASTER HANZO!!
WHA... WHAT A COINCI-DENCE...

BU...
SNIFF

I DON'T NEED ANY HELP!!
GO HOME.
LET US ACCOMPANY YOU!!
WAAAARGH
BUT WE HEARD THAT YOU WERE GOING DOWN TO AZUCHI...

HEY...
LOWER YOUR VOICE!!
FOR GOD'S SAKE...
I KIND OF FEEL SORRY FOR THEM...
DEJECTED
IT'S USA...

STUNNED
USA...
MAMEZO?!
GRAND-PA!!
WHAT A FINE DAY TODAY...

I'LL PROTECT USAGI WITH EVERYTHING I HAVE.
I PROMISE WE'LL COME BACK TO IGA SAFELY.
SO BE A GOOD BOY AND WAIT FOR US.
OKAY...
HE SAID THOSE WORDS...
...BECAUSE IT'S AN ASSIGNMENT.

USA...I'LL BE A GOOD BOY AND WAIT FOR YOU...
BOO HOO
YOU'VE GOT TO COME BACK ALIVE...

I CAN WALK!!
TMP
TMP
I...I'M FINE NOW.

SHA
GET ON.

I SHOULDN'T BE TOO DEPENDENT ON HIM!!
THIS IS AN ASSIGNMENT.
TMP
TMP

WE'RE GOING TO REST FOR THE DAY AND VISIT THE TEA PLANTATION TOMORROW.
NNKAY...
IF YOU'D LET ME CARRY YOU ON MY BACK, WE WOULD HAVE ARRIVED MUCH EARLIER!!
TROMP
WORN OUT
TROMP
I'M SORRY...
NIGHT FALLS
YOU'RE NOT FINE AT ALL.
TROMP
TROMP

YOU MUST BE TIRED FROM YOUR JOURNEY.
INN SHIMONO
DEAD TIRED
PANT
PANT
NO, THANK YOU.
WILL YOU BE HAVING DINNER?

ARE YOU TWO SIBLINGS?
SHE'S MY WIFE.

I APOLOGIZE FOR MY MISTAKE.
I SUSPECT THAT YOU'LL ONLY BE NEEDING ONE FUTON SET THEN.
Please follow me.
WHA–
JOLT
ONE FUTON WILL BE FINE.

I'M GOING TO SLEEP WITH HANZO...?!
TROMP TROMP
HURRY UP.

WELL NOW...
THIS IS A PROBLEM.

WHA...
WHAT I THINK...?
WHAT DO YOU THINK, USAGI?
Two pillows...
WE SHOULD BEHAVE MORE LIKE A MARRIED COUPLE...
MAYBE THERE'S SOMETHING I'M NOT DOING RIGHT.
E...EVEN THOUGH WE HAVE TO ACT LIKE A MARRIED COUPLE...
...IT'S TOO HARD FOR ME TO PRETEND TO BE YOUR WIFE AFTER CANCELLING OUR ENGAGEMENT...
USAGI...

I AM LOOKING AT YOU...
I...
WHY WON'T YOU LOOK AT MY EYES WHEN YOU'RE SPEAKING?
... REALLY...

I'M HANBEI.
I'M NOT HANZO.
TH-THUM.
HA... HANZO...?!
TH-THUMP

HANBEI...
FWUMP
AAH!
FOR THE SAKE OF THIS ASSIGN-MENT...
...I'M GOING TO MAKE LOVE TO YOU.

TAIL OF THE MOON EXTRA: TODAY'S MISSION

"I WANT TO SEE HANZO IN A CARPENTER'S OUTFIT!"

–"MAMEZO IS SO CUTE," SAGA PREFECTURE

Tail of the Moon
Chapter 46

TAIL OF THE MOON EXTRA: TODAY'S MISSION

"I WANT TO SEE HANZO AND HANZOU MAKING PASSES AT GIRLS!!"

-AKIZAKURA, KUMAMOTO PREFECTURE

"FOR THE SAKE OF THIS ASSIGNMENT, I'M GOING TO MAKE LOVE TO YOU."

NOT AS HANZO...
...BUT AS HANBEI ...?!
!!

NO!
BUT HE DOESN'T HAVE ANY FEELINGS FOR ME.
"THIS WAS AN UNWANTED ENGAGEMENT FOR ME FROM THE START."
NOOO!
CAN HANZO DO SUCH A THING IF IT'S FOR AN ASSIGNMENT?!
SNIFF
SNIFF
ARE YOU THAT UNWILLING?

OF COURSE I'M UN-WILLING!!
THE ONE I'M IN LOVE WITH IS HANZO!!
...CAN'T CONTINUE ON THIS ASSIGNMENT... ANYMORE.
I...

USAGI...
...BUT I CAN'T BE THAT WAY...
YOU MAY BE PERFECT AT EVERY-THING...
HANZO...
I'M...
...PERFECT?!

A PERFECT PERSON...
I REGRET WHAT I DID...
...WOULDN'T HAVE ACCEPTED MASTER TANBA'S REQUEST TO CANCEL THE ENGAGEMENT.

I'M SORRY...
...I MADE THINGS PAINFUL FOR YOU, USAGI.
THERE WAS A TIME...
...WHEN I THOUGHT IT WOULD BE BETTER FOR YOU TO MARRY GOEMON...
THAT...
BUT...

...I'M THE ONE SUITED TO MARRY YOU, USAGI!!

ONCE THIS ASSIGNMENT IS OVER, I'LL PROPOSE TO YOU AGAIN.
PROPOSE...
DO YOU MIND...
...IF I HOLD YOU?

HUG
SURE!!
HEY...
I LOVE YOU!!
THUD

I LOVE YOU.
I REALLY LOVE YOU.
IF YOU'RE SCARED...
...YOU DON'T HAVE TO GO TO AZUCHI, YOU KNOW.
I'M GOING!!

I'M GOING TO FULFILL THIS MISSION...
...GET MY QUALIFICATION...
...AND BECOME YOUR WIFE, HANZO.
IS THAT RIGHT...

FWIP
I'M EMBAR-RASSED... ♡
TEE HEE
DOES SOMEONE IN THIS POSITION GET EMBAR-RASSED?
DO YOU MIND...
...IF I STAY LIKE THIS A LITTLE LONGER?
HMM...
SURE...
I WANT TO CHERISH THIS MOMENT...
...OF FEELING CONNECTED TO HANZO...

UH...
THROB THROB
MY RATIONALITY IS...
...FALLING APART...!!
OH NO...
HANZO...
I LOVE YOU...
SNAP
URK!
GRAB
LET'S CONTINUE WITH WHAT WE WERE GOING TO DO...
USAGI...

ZZZ...
...
ZZZ...
HM
OH WELL...
YOU REALLY ARE CUTE...
PANT
PANT
DON'T...
AH...

SLAM
NO...
I'M NOT READY YET.
WAKE UP!
IT'S MORNING!
AAAH!
HUH...?
HEY!
WA... WAS THAT...
...A DREAM?!
WHAT KIND OF DREAM WAS IT?
LAST NIGHT, HANZO MADE ADVANCEMENTS TOWARD ME...
I REMEMBER!!
...AND THIS AND THAT HAPPENED...
WAAAARGH!
I DON'T KNOW!!
WHY DID I FALL ASLEEP...?!
Hurry up and get ready to leave!!

THANKS FOR EVERYTHING.
INN SHIMO
TAKE CARE...
OH...
EXCUSE ME...
DID YOU FORGET YOUR SWORD?
SPACEY
SPACEY
I NEVER HAD ONE FROM THE START.
IS THAT SO?
I COMPLETELY ASSUMED THAT YOU WERE A SAMURAI OR SOMETHING...
WHAT?!
CRNCH
THIS IS A PROBLEM...
CRNCH
USAGI...
DON'T I LOOK LIKE A MAN WHO RUNS A TEA PLANTATION?
WHAAAAAT?
DID YOU SAY SOMETHING...?
WHEEZE
WHEEZE
!!
DOES YOUR LEG STILL HURT?!

BUT...
...THE INN KEEPER ISN'T OUR ENEMY...
ONCE YOU TAKE A STEP OUT OF IGA, YOU'RE IN ENEMY TERRITORY.
PANT
PANT
TROMP
TROMP
...BUT I HAVEN'T EATEN BREAKFAST SO I'M STARVING...
MY...MY LEG'S FINE NOW...
WOBBLE
WOBBLE
NINJA ARE NOT SUPPOSED TO EAT ANYTHING GIVEN TO THEM BY OTHERS OUTSIDE OF THEIR TERRITORY.
HANZO...
I THOUGHT OUR FEELINGS FOR EACH OTHER WERE MUTUAL AT LAST, BUT HE'S THE SAME AS USUAL.
IN ORDER TO PROTECT THE INDEPENDENCE OF IGA, WE MUST SNEAK INTO AZUCHI.
HE'S GOT HIS "WORK" FACE ON...
IF YOU'RE HUNGRY, HAVE A HUNGER PILL.
HUFF
HUFF
SAY "AAAH."
BUT THEY DON'T TASTE GOOD...
HUFF...

MUNCH MUNCH
THAT SHOULD KEEP YOU GOING FOR THE DAY.
TOSS
AAAH?
WHAT'S THE MATTER?
JUST NOW, THAT LOOKED...
...AS IF WE REALLY WERE MARRIED... ♡
Daze...
RE...
...REALLY?
YOU SHOULD GET SERIOUS AND BE ON YOUR GUARD!!
WE'RE NOT GOING ON THIS TRIP FOR PLEASURE, YOU KNOW.
WAAAARGH
DON'T BE STUPID.
YOU CAN ONLY HAVE ONE PER DAY.
MORE, MORE...
AAAH! ♡
CHIRP
CHIRP

SNIFF
HMM...
BUT NORMAL MARRIED COUPLES DON'T WALK AROUND TOGETHER LOOKING SERIOUS WITH THEIR GUARDS UP...
YOU'RE RIGHT.
YOU'VE SAID SOMETHING PROPER FOR ONCE, USAGI.
GLING
HA! ♡
HE PRAISED ME.
DON'T GET CARRIED AWAY!
GRIN
I KNOW...
...HANBEI. ♡
HUMPH
WHO ARE YOU CALLING HANBEI...?
OH
IT'S HANBEI, ISN'T IT?
TH... THAT'S RIGHT.
?
NOW I KNOW HOW USAGI FEELS...

UE-RIN'S WAY OF THE MANGA ⑧

Back then, I was on the swimming team, so I would swim about 3km everyday after school, go to sleep right after coming home, and draw my manga in the middle of the night after my family members had all gone to bed.

I was really busy with my classes, extracurricular activities, and cram school, so finding time to draw manga was hard. I would draw manga happily until it was time for me to go to school.

(This was around the time I got hooked on the radio.)

I also came up with a plan to improve my skills.

Plan ①

Overcome my weak points in focus lines and shadowing!

Plan ②

Draw a 30-page one-shot manga every month and submit them to magazines.

Well, I only had two plans...

IT'S THE REMAINS FROM A FIRE.
SHA
SWISH
FUWA
WHOA!
IT SEEMS TO HAVE BEEN A TEMPLE.

TUP
WOOSH
YOU MUSTN'T DODGE IT.
WHA...
WHAT IS IT?!
EEEK
RIKIMARU?!
LONG TIME NO SEE.

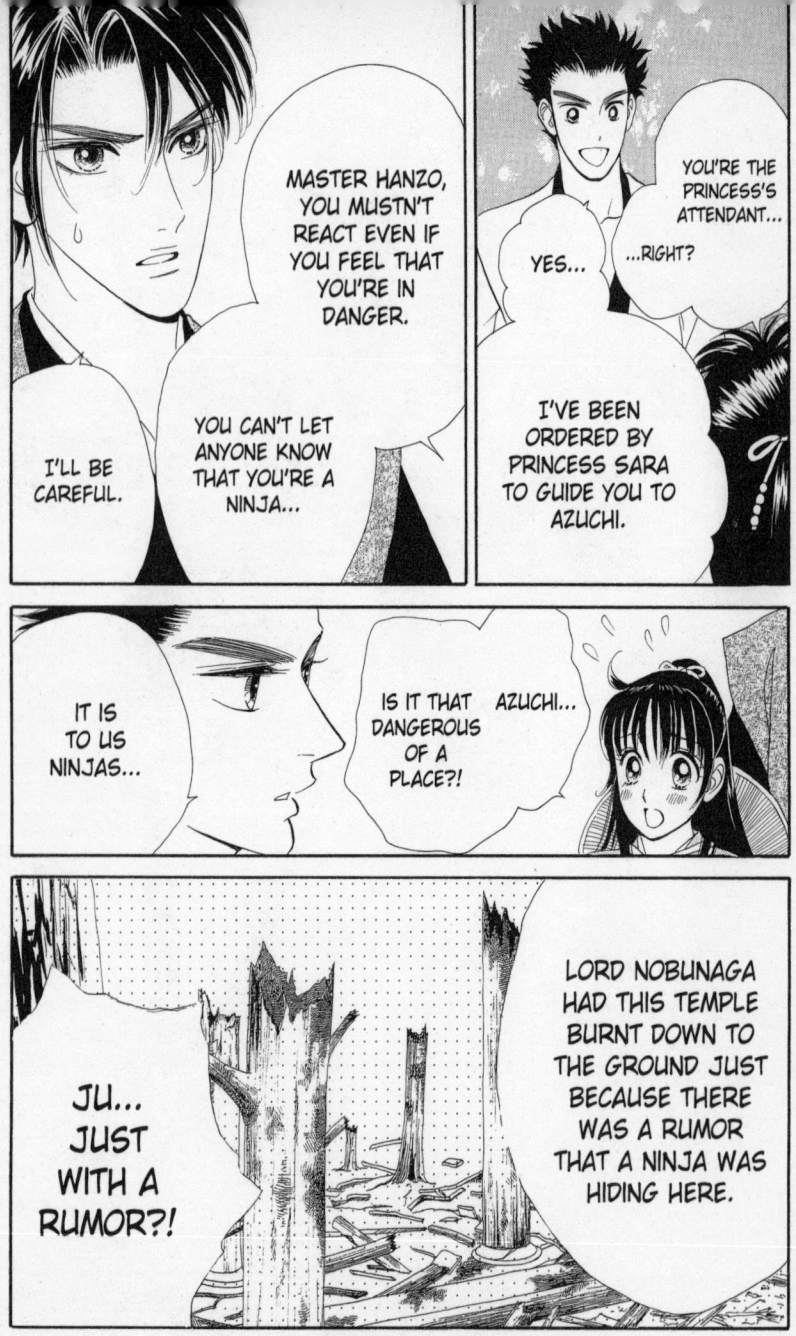
MASTER HANZO, YOU MUSTN'T REACT EVEN IF YOU FEEL THAT YOU'RE IN DANGER.
YOU CAN'T LET ANYONE KNOW THAT YOU'RE A NINJA...
I'LL BE CAREFUL.
YOU'RE THE PRINCESS'S ATTENDANT...
...RIGHT?
YES...
I'VE BEEN ORDERED BY PRINCESS SARA TO GUIDE YOU TO AZUCHI.
IT IS TO US NINJAS...
IS IT THAT DANGEROUS OF A PLACE?!
AZUCHI...
JU... JUST WITH A RUMOR?!
LORD NOBUNAGA HAD THIS TEMPLE BURNT DOWN TO THE GROUND JUST BECAUSE THERE WAS A RUMOR THAT A NINJA WAS HIDING HERE.

A NINJA TRIED TO ASSASSINATE LORD NOBUNAGA JUST A LITTLE WHILE AGO...
...SO HIS DISLIKE OF NINJA IS AT ITS PEAK RIGHT NOW.
THAT'S WHY YOU MUST BE EXTREMELY CAREFUL WHEN YOU ENTER AZUCHI.

TAIL OF THE MOON EXTRA: TODAY'S MISSION

"I WANT TO SEE USAGI AND YURI AS SCHOOL GIRLS."

-MIKAN, WAKAYAMA PREFECTURE

THE ERASER CRUMBS FROM A PLASTIC ERASER ARE NON-BURNABLE TRASH.
HANZO' TRIVIA
Tail of the Moon
Chapter 47

LORD NOBUNAGA'S DISLIKE OF NINJA IS AT ITS PEAK RIGHT NOW.
IF HE FINDS OUT THAT WE'RE NINJA, THEN...
SQUEEZE
DON'T WORRY.
HANZO...

YOU DON'T LOOK LIKE A NINJA AT ALL, USAGI.
ACTUALLY, MASTER HANZO, IT'S YOU THAT I'M WORRIED ABOUT...
UH...

WHAT?!

ARE YOU TELLING ME THAT I DON'T LOOK LIKE A PEASANT WHO WORKS ON A TEA PLANTATION?
You're scaring me...
HA... HARDLY...
CRNCH
THERE'S NO SUCH THING AS A PEASANT WITH BLOODTHIRSTY-LOOKING EYES, HANZO.

HANZOU?!
I'VE BEEN SO WORRIED ABOUT LEAVING THIS TASK IN YOUR HANDS THAT I HAVEN'T BEEN ABLE TO SLEEP.
HANZOU, YOUR CLOTHES...
ANOTHER NUISANCE.
TMP
I CAN'T MEET LORD NOBUNAGA IN MY USUAL ATTIRE, NOW CAN I?
HANZO.
HERE.
TMP

SHHK
YOU'RE GOING TO POSE AS A SAMURAI FROM OKAZAKI.
SAMURAI?
HANBEI IS A DISTANT RELATIVE OF MINE, AND YOU WORK UNDER ME.
THAT SOUNDS LIKE A MORE FEASIBLE STORY, DOESN'T IT?

WHY DO I HAVE TO BE WORKING UNDER YOU?!
GLARE
HE'S EVEN MORE BLOOD-THIRSTY NOW.
THAT'S THE BEST STORY I COULD THINK OF. IT SOUNDS MORE NATURAL.

NO...
YOU DIDN'T?!
WAIT, I WAS SUPPOSED TO BRING SOME-THING?

AT THE VERY LEAST, I SHOULD BE YOUR EQUAL!!
OH, USAGI...
DID YOU BRING YOUR TEA TO GIVE TO LORD NOBUNAGA AS A GIFT?
Stop it, please...
SHHK
GIFT?

Were you seriously going to meet Lord Nobunaga empty-handed...?!
BUT WE FINISHED ALL THE TEA BACK IN IGA!
WE CAN JUST GO BACK AND GET IT.
ARGH
WHA... WHAT SHOULD I DO...

I...I'LL MAKE SOME RIGHT NOW.
WHAAAAAT...?!

WASN'T YOUR TEA MADE FROM GREEN-TEA LEAVES?
NO...
I JUST MIXED A BUNCH OF HERBS AND SOME RANDOM GRASS.

UHHH...
We're near Uji, right?!
RIKIMARU!
WHERE'S THE CLOSEST TEA PLANTATION?
IT'S OKAY.
I'LL JUST USE THE GRASS AROUND HERE.
PICK
PICK

UE-RIN'S WAY OF THE MANGA 9

I had a lot of fun drawing focus lines and shadowing, but I had to practice hard every day to overcome my "I don't like it because I'm not good at it" sentiment.

I kept my promise of sending in one manga per month, and I finally received a small award around my third work. Gradually, I began to toddle up the thin "Manga Path" with the help of a supervisor.

Back then, the editor in charge of "Manga School" visited Osaka and decided to hold a meeting with several of the people in the Kansai region who had submitted their work. So for the first time, I went to the Big city of Osaka from the Great countryside of Nara. Alhough it was a prefecture right next to mine (well, a city), Osaka felt like a huge metropolis that was far, far away.

THE NEXT DAY
I'M GLAD YOU WERE ABLE TO MAKE THE TEA!
OH, WE'RE ALMOST AT AZUCHI.
OH... ALREADY?
WOBBLE WOBBLE
IF NOBUNAGA WERE TO ATTACK WITH A LARGE ARMY, THEY WOULD REACH US IN SECONDS.
AZUCHI AND IGA ARE VERY CLOSE TO EACH OTHER WITH ONLY KOUGA IN-BETWEEN THEM.
IF THAT EVER HAPPENS, THEN IGA WILL...
THAT IS WHY WE'RE GOING TO AZUCHI, SO THAT IT WILL NEVER HAPPEN.
DON'T WORRY.
HANZO...
THEY'RE IN THEIR OWN WORLD.
LOOK, RIKIMARU.
Ah.

HUG
SHIVER
A REAL ...?
I'M SO GLAD, HANZO...
I WAS BEING HAPPY FOR YOU!!
HANZOU ...!
IF WE DON'T HURRY, THEY'RE GOING TO LEAVE US BEHIND.
RIGHT.
AAAAAH...
A REAL HUSBAND AND WIFE ...
SAY WHAT YOU WANT.
ONCE THIS ASSIGNMENT IS OVER, USAGI AND I WILL BE A REAL HUSBAND AND WIFE.

I'M GOING TO HAVE TO DO MY BEST ON THIS ASSIGNMENT!!
SO THIS IS AZUCHI?
I'VE NEVER SEEN SUCH A LARGE TOWN.
GANK
GANK
DON'T GAPE WITH YOUR MOUTH OPEN.
OH

OOH!!
WHAT IS THAT, A TOY SHOP?!
SHAKE
SHAKE
OH
SEE, I KNEW YOU NEEDED ME.
I...I MEAN, HANBEI ...
CLAP
HANZO, LOOK, LOOK!
A DUMPLING SHOP!!
YOU CALLED?
LOOK, THERE'S A SHOP THAT SELLS YOUR FAVORITE ANTIQUES.
IF IT'S GOING TO HELP EASE HER TENSION, WHY NOT LET HER?
WE DIDN'T COME HERE TO PLAY...
CAN I GO AND GET A SOUVENIR FOR MAMEZO?
HANBEI, DID YOU FIND SOMETHING YOU LIKE?
ITS BLACK IRON-LIKE COLOR IS SO BEAUTIFUL!!
YOU HAVE GREAT TASTE SIR!!
CLAMP
I'LL TAKE IT...
THAT'S...
...A SETOGURO TEA BOWL!!
DON'T TREAT ME LIKE I'M HER...

NOT A CHANCE.
BUT I GRABBED IT BEFORE YOU DID.
TUG
TUG
I'M SORRY, BUT I HAD MY EYE ON THIS TEA BOWL BEFORE YOU DID.
HEY...
BUT MISTER, HE WAS HERE BEFORE YOU, WASN'T HE?
IT'S NONE OF YOUR BUSINESS!!
OWW
SHOVE
WHA... WHAT ARE YOU GOING TO DO?!
GRR
GRR
I CANNOT LET THIS TEA BOWL FALL INTO THE HANDS OF A MAN LIKE HIM!!
NO, I WON'T.
JUST GIVE THE TEA BOWL TO THAT OLD MAN.
HOW DARE YOU TREAT MY WIFE LIKE THAT!
YOU...

WE'LL FIGHT IT OUT OVER ROCK-PAPER-SCISSORS!!
THUD
STOP IT!
THIS!!
VERY WELL.
GOOD LUCK, HANBEI...
DO WHAT YOU WANT!
ROCK... PAPER...
LET'S START!!
...SCISSORS!!
FWOP
SHHK
GRP
I WI...
GOOD!
WELL, I'M NOT GOING TO LOSE AGAINST A PUP LIKE YOU.
LET ME TELL YOU THAT I HAVE NEVER LOST IN A GAME OF ROCK-PAPER-SCISSORS.

YOU'RE DRAWING ATTENTION.
STOP IT.
I WON'T ALLOW THIS...
HOW MUCH IS IT?
UM...
I FEEL SO SORRY FOR HANZO...
HA HA HA
YOU CHEATER !!
I'M THE WINNER!!
I WIN!
GRRRR
BUT YOU CHEATED!!
HANBEI...
HOW UN-PLEASANT...
WHAT A FINE TEA BOWL!!
HA HA HA...
IT'S A PRESENT FROM ME TO YOU, HANBEI. ♡
I WAS TOLD THAT THIS IS OLDER THAN THAT TEA BOWL...
WHAT?!
HUFF HUFF

IT'S CALLED A DOGU. ♡
SHUP

FOR ME...?
DOGU?

USAGI!!
I'LL TAKE GOOD CARE OF IT.
WHAT HAPPENED BETWEEN YOU AND HANZO?!
SNEAK

I LIKE IT A LOT.
I'M SO GLAD...
...THAT YOU LIKE IT. ♡
HUH?!

USAGI...
GET AWAY FROM THAT WALKING OBSCENITY AND COME CLOSER TO ME.
USAGI'S GOT THE FACE OF A WOMAN...
Did it happen at last?!
OKAY!
I CAN'T TALK ABOUT...
...SUCH THINGS...
!!
DON'T LEAVE MY SIDE.
OOH...

I WANT TO PROTECT...
HEY, NEWLY-WEDS...
WHY DON'T YOU DROP BY OUR PLACE?
IS SHE TALKING ABOUT US...?
...THIS HAPPY FEELING...

THIS...
...IS AZUCHI CASTLE.

...GOLDEN WALLS...
...CRIMSON PILLARS...
A LONG FLIGHT OF STONE STEPS THAT SEEM TO REACH UP TO THE SKY...
AND ON TOP OF THAT...
IT'S A CASTLE FIT FOR A GOD TO LIVE IN.

USAGI!
WE'RE GOING TO FIND AN INN.
OH!
I...INN?!
LORD NOBUNAGA'S OUT FOR TWO TO THREE DAYS, SO WE HAVE TO COME BACK LATER.
THANK GOD...
PHEW
HANZOU...
TWITCH
...WE'D NEVER BE ABLE TO WIN.
IF WE GO TO WAR WITH NOBUNAGA, A MAN WHO HAS THE POWER TO BUILD SUCH AN AMAZING CASTLE...
...SAGI...

PRINCESS...?
SHE'S SARA'S OLDER SISTER.
LONG TIME NO SEE, HANZOU.
PRINCESS TOKU!
SO YOU'RE THE ONE WHO MADE THAT TEA?
YE...
...YES!!
EEEEEEEEK... I CAN'T BELIEVE I'M INSIDE AZUCHI CASTLE...
U... USAGI!!
AND WHAT IS YOUR NAME?

USAGI?
WHAT A CUTE NAME.
SHE'S GOT SUCH A CLEAR, BEAUTIFUL VOICE...
SHE'S PRETTY, ELEGANT, AND HAS FLOWING HAIR...
SHE'S TOTALLY HANZO'S TYPE OF WOMAN...
AND YOU, SIR?
I'M HANBEI, USAGI'S HUSBAND.
HE'S A DISTANT RELATIVE OF MINE WHO WORKS WITH ME AT OKAZAKI CASTLE.
THROB
HUSBAND... ♡

YOU MUST BE TIRED, HAVING COME ALL THIS WAY FROM OKAZAKI.
I'LL HAVE SOME TEA PREPARED RIGHT AWAY.
I'VE BROUGHT SOME TEA AS A GIFT...
IT'S NOT THAT KIND OF TEA, USAGI.
OH, I'M SO THRILLED.
I GET TO HAVE SOME OF THAT DELICIOUS TEA THEN.
THE TEA MASTER'S HERE TODAY, SO I'LL HAVE HIM MAKE US SOME TEA.
HUH?
THAT TEA BOWL...
SHHK

HOW DO YOU DO.
I'M...
HUH!
YOU...!!
IT'S THAT OLD CHEATER WE JUST MET!!
SO YOU'RE THE GUESTS I WAS TOLD ABOUT.
DO YOU KNOW EACH OTHER?
THIS OLD MAN...
THANK YOU VERY MUCH FOR LETTING ME HAVE THE SETOGURO TEA BOWL.
I'M SEN NO RIKYU...LORD NOBUNAGA'S TEA MASTER.

I'M SORRY, BUT I CANNOT DO THAT.
HUMPH
CAN YOU MAKE SOME TEA FOR THESE GUESTS FROM OKAZAKI?
RIKYU...
THIS CHEATING OLD MAN IS A TEA MASTER?!
RIKYU...?!
THAT MAN IS NOT A SAMURAI FROM OKAZAKI.
PRINCESS TOKU...

TAIL OF THE MOON EXTRA: TODAY'S MISSION

"I WANT TO SEE HANZO AND HANZOU BABYSITTING!"

-SAORI ASAI, AICHI PREFECTURE

Tail of the Moon
Chapter 48
I CAN'T WAIT FOR LISA TO COME BACK...
TUP
TUP
PEOPLE SEEM EVEN MORE LATE WHEN YOU WAIT FOR THEM.
HANZO'S TRIVIA
THE FAMOUS HAWAIIAN SONG "ALOHAOE" ACTUALLY COMES FROM AN AUSTRIAN FOLK SONG.

THAT MAN IS NOT A SAMURAI FROM OKAZAKI.

HAS HE DISCOVERED THAT WE'RE NINJA?!
WHY DO YOU SAY THAT?
I WOULD HAVE NOTICED SUCH A RUDE SAMURAI AROUND WHEN I DROPPED BY OKAZAKI THIS SUMMER.
ACTUALLY, YOU WOULDN'T HAVE.
HANBEI GOT THIS JOB ONLY A WHILE AGO.
NICE TO MEET YOU...
HMM?!
I SEE. IS THAT SO?
THIS MAN'S SHARPER THAN I THOUGHT...
THIS OLD MAN HAD ME WORRIED FOR A SECOND...
THEN WILL YOU MAKE US SOME TEA?
SWP
IF YOU INSIST, PRINCESS TOKU...
HUMPH
I'LL MAKE THE TEA!!
SHUP SHUP
I POUR IN THE TEA LEAVES...
SHAKE SHAKE
SHAKE THE POT AROUND...
...AND POUR...
GUSH GUSH

PHEW
It looks hot.
HERE YOU ARE, PRINCESS TOKU. ♪
TH... THANK YOU.
TH...
I CANNOT ACCEPT TEA POURED BY SUCH INCORRECT METHODS!!
THAT IS INCORRECT!
SHUDDER SHUDDER
I DON'T NEED YOU TO ACCEPT IT...
YOU'RE RIGHT.
HAN-BEI...
MY WIFE IS AN AMATEUR AT BREWING TEA...
...SO IT MUST SEEM COMPLETELY INCORRECT TO A SKILLED TEA CEREMONY MASTER LIKE YOURSELF, RIKYU.

BUT IF YOU REJECT THIS TEA...
...WOULDN'T IT BE THE SAME AS MOCKING LORD NOBUNAGA SINCE HE LIKES IT?
THAT'S RIGHT, RIKYU.
YOU MUSTN'T REJECT THE TEA BEFORE EVEN TRYING IT...
PLEASE TRY IT, RIKYU.
IF YOU SAY SO, PRINCESS TOKU...
SIP
IT'S FINE!
GRR GRR
I DIDN'T MAKE IT FOR THAT OLD MAN TO DRINK...
SEE, HE DOESN'T LIKE IT...

HUH?
IT IS AN INCREDIBLY SMOOTH TEA WITH A WONDERFUL ROASTED FLAVOR TO IT!!
DELICIOUS...
MMRPH
MY WIFE HAS HAD A DEEP INTEREST IN HERBS EVER SINCE CHILDHOOD.
I WAS TRYING TO MAKE A TEA TO LOSE WEIGHT BUT FAILED...
I MADE IT MY-SELF...
WHO DID YOU LEARN THIS TEA RECIPE FROM?
HE CHANGED HIS ATTITUDE SO QUICKLY...
HA HA HA
THANK YOU VERY MUCH.
YOUR WIFE MUST BE A GENIUS TO HAVE MADE SUCH A WONDERFUL TEA FROM MERE SELF-STUDY!!

I DON'T LIKE THAT OLD MAN...
I DON'T CARE IF HE'S SOME FAMOUS TEA MASTER OR NOT...
TOSS
TOSS
THAT RIKYU IS PRETTY SHARP.
FOLD
YEAH, HE IS.
I HEAR THAT PEOPLE TALK ABOUT POLITICS AT TEA CEREMONIES.
I BET RIKYU WOULD KNOW ABOUT THE ATTACK ON IGA.
HANBEI WAS TELLING ME HOW HE WAS GOING TO PLAY WITH YOU TONIGHT. ♪
NYAAAA
I SAID NOTHING OF THE SORT!!
WELL THEN, HAVE FUUUUN... ♡
WHAT ARE YOU TWO TALKING ABOUT?
HMM?
SQUISH
LET'S JUST GO TO SLEEP, USAGI!!
TH-THUMP
CAN IT BE...
...THAT HE'S THINKING OF CONTINUING WHAT WE WERE DOING THE OTHER NIGHT...?!
TH-THUMP

SHA
HANBEI...
I'M NOT READY YET, BUT I'M WILLING TO...
THUD
ZZZ...
HE... HE FELL ASLEEP SO FAST...
ZZZ
I GUESS...
...THERE'S NO REASON TO RUSH...
ONCE THIS ASSIGNMENT IS OVER, HANZO AND I WILL BECOME A REAL HUSBAND AND WIFE.
AND I CAN EVEN RECEIVE MY QUALIFICATION FROM GREAT-GRANDPA.
THIS IS SO GREAT! ♡
I'M GOING TO DO MY BEST!!
GOOD NIGHT!

UE-RIN'S WAY OF THE MANGA 10

My best memory of meeting the editor for the first time was how I was able to take a look at a real draft of an author who had a series in the magazine back then. It was so beautiful!! "Do you have to be so detailed with the backgrounds?!" "I love these effects!!" "How can you draw the reflection of light in the eyes and hair so beautifully?!" It really was an eye-opener for me!! My confidence and pride just got flushed away and I felt really embarrassed of myself. The images I saw in the magazine and the real thing were totally different. It was ten times as beautiful...no, even more beautiful than that!!

ZZZ
CINCH
I MUST FINISH THIS ASSIGNMENT QUICKLY AND RETURN TO IGA FOR USAGI'S SAKE AS WELL...
MMPH...
KICK
HM?
OH USAGI...
TUCK

TUP
THIS CASTLE IS ENORMOUS.
I'LL NEVER FINISH LOOKING AROUND IN ONLY ONE NIGHT.

MMPH...
KICK
NGH
...
HANBEI...?
HANBEI?
TMP
TMP
HE'S NOT IN THE BATH-ROOM...
SHHK
THAT MUST BE IT.
TMP
TMP
MAYBE WE MISSED EACH OTHER, AND HE'S ALREADY BACK IN THE ROOM...
I HOPE HANZO WASN'T CAPTURED BECAUSE THEY FOUND OUT HE'S A NINJA...
OH DEAR
OH DEAR
HUH?
WHERE'S MY ROOM AGAIN?

WHAT ARE YOU DOING?
TH-THUMP
YEEARGH
I...I'M NOT A SUSPICIOUS PERSON OR ANYTHING...
I...I JUST GOT LOST...
YOU MUST BE THE ONE WHO BROUGHT THE TEA.
TH... THAT'S RIGHT...
LET ME GUIDE YOU TO YOUR ROOM THEN.
OH...
HE DOESN'T HAVE TO HOLD MY HAND...
BE CARE-FUL.
THERE'S A SMALL STEP AHEAD.
TH... THANKS.
WHIFF
OH!

HE'S A MAN...
...BUT HE SMELLS SO NICE...
I GUESS THERE ARE KIND PEOPLE EVEN AMONG NOBUNAGA'S MEN...
USAGI!!
HANZ...
HANBEI...
WHERE HAVE YOU BEEN?!
I...I WENT TO THE BATHROOM AND COULDN'T FIND MY WAY BACK.
BUT THAT MAN OVER THERE HELPED ME...
HUH?
I DIDN'T EVEN THANK HIM YET...
ZWAK
DON'T GO OUT BY YOURSELF!!

HUG
BUT HANBEI, YOU...
DO YOU ANY IDEA HOW WORRIED I WAS?!
NAG NAG NAG NAG
I DON'T UNDER-STAND SINCE HE'S SCOLDING ME BY JUST MOVING HIS LIPS...
WHERE DO YOU THINK WE ARE?! IF THEY FIND OUT THAT WE ARE NINJA...
SIT DOWN.
HANZO...
USAGI...

USAGI...
WAKE UP!!
I'M STILL SLEEEEEPY.
SMACK
GREAT VIEW... ♪
OW!
WAKE UP AND GET CHANGED!!
SNAP
LORD NOBUNAGA CAME BACK JUST A MOMENT AGO!!
WE'RE GOING TO SEE HIM NOW.
JOOM
RI... RIGHT NOW?!
IF WE'RE LATE, WHO KNOWS WHAT'LL HAPPEN TO US? ♪

BUT I'M NOT READY YET...
HURRY UP!!
PANT
PANT
HUFF
HUFF
TH... THESE STONE STEPS ARE SO TOUGH...
HUH?
AAAAAAH
WHAT'S WRONG?!
TH...THIS STONE...
...HAS BUDDHA ENGRAVED ON IT...!!
AAAAAAH

WHAT'S IT DOING HERE?!
IT'S BEEN PLACED THERE TO STOP ENEMY SOLDIERS.
BU... BUT...
...YOU'LL RECEIVE DIVINE PUNISHMENT IF YOU DO SOMETHING LIKE THIS...
JUST BE CAREFUL NOT TO STEP ON IT.
COME TO THINK OF IT, NOBUNAGA BURNED ENRYAKUJI TO THE GROUND, DIDN'T HE...
THIS IS TOO SCARY...
I'M HERE FOR YOU.

THERE'S NOTHING TO BE AFRAID OF.
HANZO'S WITH ME.
OKAY.
HE'S RIGHT NEXT TO ME...
WHAT'S THAT?
SHI
MOSUKE...!
PLEASE COME DOWN, MOSUKE.

MOSUKE...
PLEASE RETURN TO THE CASTLE...
CRASH
OW!
EEEEEK
GWAA
KEE...
A...
A MONKEY ?!
YOU...
HOW DARE YOU CALL MOSUKE A MONKEY?!
HUH?!
BUT HE'S A LARGE MONKEY, ISN'T HE?

MOSUKE IS A PERSON WHO HAS COME FROM THE WEST!!
KEE...
WHAT ?!
CRNCH
CRNCH
NO MATTER HOW YOU LOOK AT HIM, HE'S NOTHING BUT A LARGE MONKEY!!
WHAT ARE YOU TALKING ABOUT?!
Y...YOU'VE CALLED HIM A MONKEY TWICE NOW!
PLEASE STOP THAT.
GLATTER
GLATTER

SINCE LORD NOBUNAGA LOOKS UPON MOSUKE AS A MAN...
...IT IS THE DUTY OF HIS RETAINERS TO FOLLOW ALONG.
WHIFF
THIS SCENT...
MOSUKE, COME HERE...
KEE...
NO
NO
IT SEEMS LIKE MOSUKE HAS TAKEN A LIKING TO YOU.

THE MAN FROM LAST NIGHT!!
YOU KNOW HIM, USAGI?
NO.
IT'S NOT THAT I KNOW HIM, BUT...
I'M MORI RANMARU...
...LORD NOBUNAGA'S PAGE.
I DIDN'T KNOW THAT HE WAS SO BEAUTIFUL...
I COULDN'T TELL LAST NIGHT BECAUSE IT WAS SO DARK.
HMM...
I'VE GOT THIS FEELING THAT I'VE MET HIM SOMEWHERE BEFORE...
BUT I'D NEVER FORGET SOMEBODY AS BEAUTIFUL AS HIM...
YOU'RE THE FIRST PERSON I KNOW WHO'S CALLED MOSUKE A MONKEY RIGHT TO HIS FACE.

I'M SORRY...
NOT AT ALL.
I LIKE PEOPLE WHO ARE HONEST.
OH!
HUMPH
BUT IF YOU WANT TO LIVE LONGER, I ADVISE YOU TO TREAT MOSUKE AS A HUMAN BEING.
EEEEEEK
O... OKAY!

B-BUMP
PLEASE COME IN.
B-BUMP
LORD NOBUNAGA IS WAITING FOR YOU.
...I'M GOING TO MEET ODA NOBUNAGA ...!!
SO AT LONG LAST...

AN OWL'S EARS ARE NOT ALIGNED— ONE IS HIGHER THAN THE OTHER.
HANZO'S TRIVIA
Tail of the Moon
Chapter 49

I'VE BROUGHT THE GUESTS.
LORD NOBUNAGA...
B- BUMP B- BUMP
B- BUMP B- BUMP

...ODA NOBUNAGA !!
...SEE.
I...
SO THIS IS...
!!
GASP
HE'S OVER-WHELMING.
IT FEELS LIKE HE'LL KILL ME IF OUR EYES EVEN MEET...
WHAT ARE YOU DOING?!
HE'S OVER-WHELMING AND SCARY.

LORD NOBUNAGA DOES NOT GREET HIS GUESTS WITH HIS BACK TO THEM.
AAAH... I'M SORRY...
I...I'M SORRY.
BUT LAST TIME, I SAW HIM GREET HIS GUEST THIS WAY...
KNEEL
THAT'S BECAUSE IT WAS A CLOUDY DAY!!
?!

WHAT'S GOING ON?!
HANZOU, THAT'S...
DON'T!
USAGI...
STOP IT!
GRAB
IF YOU DO SOMETHING LIKE THAT TO LORD NOBUNAGA, HE'LL KILL YOU.
TREMBLE
TREMBLE
USAGI...
THIS MAN IS LORD NOBUNAGA'S BODY DOUBLE.

BODY...
...DOUBLE?
LORD NOBUNAGA IS CURRENTLY BUSY WITH A WAR COUNCIL, SO WE DECIDED TO USE A BODY DOUBLE...
A WAR COUNCIL?!
IT COULD BE ABOUT AN ATTACK ON IGA...
...BUT I AM DREADFULLY SORRY TO HAVE GOTTEN SUCH AN UNSKILLED BODY DOUBLE. EVEN HANBEI SAW THROUGH HIM.
HANBEI, YOU COULD TELL?
HE'S PRETTY SHARP...

TROMP
TROMP
BEFORE YOU GO, I'VE BEEN ORDERED TO GIVE YOU A GIFT.
GIFT?!
WILL THE OTHERS PLEASE WAIT HERE?
BUT...
I'M SO GLAD... NOW I CAN GO BACK TO IGA ALIVE.
TH...THEN THE REAL LORD NOBUNAGA...?
UNFORTUNATELY, YOU WON'T BE ABLE TO MEET HIM.
SO I CAN GO HOME NOW?!
DON'T WORRY.
I'M NOT GOING TO EAT YOUR WIFE OR ANYTHING.
HUMPH...
HANBEI...
YOU'VE GOT REALLY DEEP SCOWL LINES BETWEEN YOUR EYES...
You're scaring me...

USAGI...
PLEASE FOLLOW ME...
TMP
TMP
THESE ARE LORD NOBUNAGA'S TREASURES.
PLEASE CHOOSE ANY ITEM YOU WOULD LIKE TO KEEP AS A GIFT.
IT'S DAZZLING...
WOW...

WHAT'S THIS ROUND THING?
They're all so glitzy...
IT'S REALLY NICE TO BE ABLE TO CHOOSE ANY ONE OF THEM, BUT I CAN'T TELL WHAT THEY ARE...
THIS IS A GLOBE. IT'S A THREE-DIMENSIONAL MAP OF THE STAR WE LIVE ON.
MAR
MARE PAC
WE...
...WE LIVE ON A STAR?!
I'VE BEEN TOLD THAT THIS WORLD IS A ROUND STAR LIKE THE MOON AND THE SUN.
OOOH, I NEVER KNEW THAT.
Wow...it rotates too...
WONDER-FUL...!!
HUH?
YOU AND LORD NOBUNAGA ARE THE ONLY PEOPLE I KNOW WHO HAVE BEEN ABLE TO ACCEPT THIS WORLD AS BEING ROUND SO QUICKLY!!
OH... REALLY?

SO ON THIS MAP, WHERE ARE THE CITIES?
THE CITIES ARE TOO SMALL TO BE WRITTEN HERE...
...BUT THIS IS JAPAN, WHERE WE LIVE.
AND IF WE ROTATE THIS GLOBE HALF WAY, WE GET TO THE WEST, WHERE THIS GLOBE IS FROM.
SO YUKI'S GONE TO A PLACE THAT'S REALLY FAR AWAY.
YUKI?
A FRIEND FROM OKAZAKI WHO WENT TO THE WEST TO STUDY.
THAT'S NICE.
I WOULD LIKE TO GO TO THE WEST SOMEDAY, TOO.

THIS PROFILE...
I'M SURE I'VE SEEN IT SOMEWHERE BEFORE...
OOH, OUR EYES MET.
LET'S SEE, WHAT SHOULD I CHOOSE...
SWIP
KEE...
WHAT'S THAT?
IT'S SO SHINY.
MOSUKE, NO!!

THIS IS A CUP MADE FROM THE SKULL OF LORD ASAI NAGAMASA. IT IS THE ONE THING I CANNOT GIVE YOU.
I'M SORRY...
SKULL...?
YOU MUSTN'T PLAY WITH THE SKULL!!
SNATCH
A...
...A CUP MADE FROM A SKULL...?!
...BUT HE HAD A GOLDEN CUP MADE OUT OF HIS SKULL AS WELL...
LORD NAGAMASA WOULD NEVER HAVE ENDED UP LIKE THIS IF HE HADN'T REBELLED AGAINST LORD NOBUNAGA...
NOT ONLY DID NOBUNAGA KILL HIM...

UE-RIN'S WAY OF THE MANGA (11)

During the meeting, I brought along two 30-page manga pieces that I created during my summer vacation to prove to the editor that "this middle schooler's really trying hard."
I had the editor look through my work and give me advice about it, but in the end, I was so nervous that I didn't remember anything I was told.
Argh...I should have taken notes...
I'm really sorry that my sentences are hard to read since I'm writing them down as I remember them off the top of my head. And since this is the last column in this volume, I'll write the rest in the next volume!

Send your messages and letters to the address below. We're looking forward to your requests for the Extra Missions as well!

Rinko Ueda
C/O Shojo Beat
Viz Media
P.O. Box 77010
San Francisco, CA
94107

Rinko Ueda

SPARKLE
SPARKLE
I'M REALLY SORRY TO HAVE TALKED ABOUT THE SKULL...
"HELLO, MY ANGEL."
DAZZLING...
USAGI?
WHY DID HIKARU SUDDENLY COME TO MIND...?
!!

"THAT PERSON WAS SO GOOD-LOOKING..."
THIS GUY...
HE'S THE ONE I SAW AT KOUGA...!!

I HAVE TO ESCAPE.
EEEEEEK
YOUR FACE IS REALLY PALE.
QUIVER
SLIP
FONK
OW!
IF HE REMEMBERS ME...
CALM DOWN, USAGI.
OWWW...
...THEN HE KNOWS THAT I'M A NINJA!!

IF HE DID REMEMBER, I GUESS HE WOULD HAVE CAUGHT ME BY NOW...
HE DOESN'T REMEMBER ...?
THERE'S NOTHING TO WORRY ABOUT...
KEE...
AND I'M WEARING A DISGUISE, TOO...
I'M...
...FINE...
!!
TUG
...SO HE WON'T NOTICE.

HMM?
USAGI, YOUR HAIR...
KEE?
SHHF
KEE!
MY WIG...!!

GIVE IT BACK!
YANK
OH, NO!
KEE?
HE'S NOTICED FOR SURE...
...
USAGI...
IT'S ALL OR NOTHING NOW...
PLEASE!!
DON'T TELL ANYBODY ABOUT THE WIG!!
THIS IS, WELL...
I TRIED TO CUT MY OWN HAIR AND FAILED...
BUT HANBEI LIKES LONG HAIR, SO...
PLEASE...

WE SHOULD RETURN SOON, OR YOUR FRIENDS ARE GOING TO BE WORRIED ABOUT YOU.
HAVE YOU DECIDED ON A GIFT?
I JUST WANT TO GO BACK TO IGA...
OH, I REALLY DON'T WANT ANYTHING.
YOU'RE BEING TOO MODEST.
WHY NOT TAKE THIS GLOBE BACK WITH YOU?
TH... THANK YOU...
HE BELIEVED IT?!
VERY WELL.
THIS WILL BE A SECRET BETWEEN THE TWO OF US.

I HAVE TO TELL HANZO THAT I SAW HIM AT KOUGA.

WHY DIDN'T YOU NOTICE SUCH AN IMPORTANT THING EARLIER?!
YOU IDIOT!!
BUT IF I TELL HIM...

BAM
IF THAT HAPPENS, I...
HANZO...
FORGET ABOUT THE MARRIAGE !!
A KLUTZ LIKE YOU WILL NEVER BE ABLE TO QUALIFY AS A NINJA.
WAAAAGH
TROMP
TROMP

LUCKILY, RANMARU DOESN'T SEEM TO HAVE NOTICED ME...
I DON'T WANT THAT TO HAPPEN...

SO I'LL JUST KEEP QUIET...

WHAT TOOK YOU SO LONG?!
TMP
TMP

SHE WAS TAKING HER TIME CHOOSING A GIFT...
TH... THAT'S RIGHT.
I DECIDED TO HAVE THIS ROUND THING...
HEE
USAGI...
YOUR HAIR IS A MESS.
B-BUMP
OH, REALLY?
WERE YOU REALLY JUST TAKING YOUR TIME CHOOSING A GIFT?!
UH... UH-HUH...
CHUCKLE
CHUCKLE
WHAT'S SO FUNNY?
I CAN'T TELL YOU.
IT'S A SECRET BETWEEN ME AND USAGI.

I have to bring this under control...
DID HE HAVE TO SAY IT IN SUCH A SECRETIVE WAY...?
CHUCKLE CHUCKLE
W...WE'LL BE LEAVING NOW TO RETURN TO OKAZAKI.
OH!
A SECRET?
THAT'S RIGHT. WE HAVE TO HURRY BACK AND REPORT THIS TO LORD IEYASU.
OKAZAKI ?!
WE'RE SUPPOSED TO BE FROM OKAZAKI.
OH, RIGHT...
AND ONCE WE'RE BACK IN IGA, I'LL HAVE MY WEDDING WITH HANZO...
BUT ALL WE HAVE TO DO IS PRETEND TO GO TO OKAZAKI AND RETURN TO IGA INSTEAD.
A SECRET...
WHAT SECRET...?!
I'LL ACCOMPANY YOU.

TO BE CONTINUED...

The ways of the ninja are mysterious indeed, so here is a glossary of terms to help you navigate the intricacies of their world.

Page 32: **Bae Yong Joon**
Bae Yong Joon is the leading actor in *Winter Sonata*.

Page 35, panel 2: **Nanmaida**
Nanmaida is the shortened form of *Namu-amidabutsu*, which means "Hail Amida-buddha." It's a prayer from Pure Land Buddhism, and it's probably one of the most famous Buddhist prayers in Japan.

Page 49, panel 8: **Princess**
Sara is not a princess in the European sense of the word. The Japanese word *hime* means a young woman of noble birth.

Page 49, panel 8: **Oda Nobunaga**
Nobunaga lived from 1534 to 1582, and came close to unifying Japan. He is probably one of the most famous Japanese warlords. He was the first warlord to successfully incorporate the gun in battle, and is notorious for his ruthlessness. He completely razed Mt. Hiei, a major Japanese Buddhist site of the time, and spared no lives in the battle.

Page 50, panel 1: **Azuchi**
Azuchi is on Lake Biwa in Shiga Prefecture, where Nobunaga built his castle and the town that were the center of his operations.

Page 58: **108 Earthly Desires**
Buddhists believe that humans have 108 earthly desires (though the number actually differs from sect to sect). That's why monks toll the bell 108 times on New Year's Eve to get rid of those desires.

Page 2: **Shimo no Hanzo**
Shimo no means "the Lower," and in this case refers to Hanzo's geographic location rather than social status.

Page 2: **Ninjutsu**
Ninjutsu means the skill or ability of a ninja.

Page 2: **Iga**
Iga is a region on the island of Honshu and also the name of the famous ninja clan that originated there. Another area famous for its ninja is Kouga, in the Shiga prefecture on Honshu. Many books claim that these two ninja clans were mortal enemies, but in reality inter-ninja relations were not as bad as stories might suggest.

Page 13, panel 3: **Manga School**
"Manga School" is a section in Japanese manga magazines for people who want to become manga artists. Participants who receive high scores for their sample manga submissions get an award along with a chance to make their debut in the magazine.

Page 32: **Winter Sonata**
Winter Sonata is a famous Korean TV drama series that was a big hit in Korea. It then became a huge hit in Japan, essentially starting the recent Korean drama/movie craze in Japan.

Page 127, panel 1: Dogu
Dogu are clay figurines that were made during the Jomon period of ancient Japan. Their purpose still remains unclear, but they were most likely used as effigies to which people could transfer illnesses and then destroy, clearing that person of that illness or misfortune.

Page 136, panel 4: Sen no Rikyu
Sen no Rikyu (1522-1591) is famous for having a huge influence on the Japanese tea ceremony, particularly in wabi-cha (a style that emphasizes simplicity). Rikyu became tea master for Oda Nobunaga when he was 58 years old.

Page 156, panel 3: Enryakuji
Enryakuji is a famous temple on Mt. Hiei and was a pretty significant symbol of Buddhism at the time. Because the Buddhists did not obey Nobunaga, he burned the temple to the ground in 1571, killing 20 to 30 thousand men, women, and children in the process.

Page 161, panel 2: Ranmaru Mori
Ranmaru Mori is one of Nobunaga's most famous vassals. He became Oda Nobunaga's attendant at a young age and was recognized for his talent and loyalty.

Page 176, panel 3: Asai Nagamasa
Asai Nagamasa (1545-1573) was the lord of Omi and also Oda Nobunaga's brother-in-law. He chose to join the Asakura family and the monks of Mt. Hiei against Nobunaga and was killed as a result.

Page 188, panel 2: Tokugawa Ieyasu
Tokugawa Ieyasu (1543-1616) was the first Shogun of the Tokugawa Shogunate. He made a small fishing village named Edo the center of his activities. Edo thrived and became a huge town, and was later renamed Tokyo, the present capital.

Page 59: Kanto vs. Kansai
The Kanto region is to the east of Honshu and is made up of seven prefectures: Gunma, Tochigi, Ibaraki, Saitama, Tokyo, Chiba, and Kanagawa. The Kansai region is to the west of Honshu and is made up of Nara, Wakayama, Mie, Kyoto, Osaka, Hyogo, and Shiga. The cultures of the two regions are often compared because of the differences in food, manners, accents, etc.

Page 71, panel 1: Uji
Uji is an area in Japan famous for its green tea.

Page 72, panel 7: Jizo
Jizo are considered the guardian deities of children. However, Jizo statues are also placed alongside travel paths throughout Japan, acting as guardians to those who travel on such paths.

Page 86: Kunoichi
A term often used for female ninja. The word is spelled くノー, and when combined, the letters form the kanji for woman, 女。

Page 112: Purikura
Purikura are photo stickers taken inside photo booth machines found in arcades and other places in Japan. Once the picture is taken, the subjects can customize and decorate the photo using a pen-sensitive touch-screen.

Page 117, panel 1: Okazaki
Okazaki is in Aichi prefecture on the main island of Honshu, about 22 miles from Nagoya.

This is the first volume in which Hanzo actually acts like a ninja. Even though *Tail of the Moon* is a ninja manga, you don't really see a lot of ninja action. These days, I'm trying to go against the "This is _____, so it must be like _____" rule since it only limits the freedom of my imagination. I hope to continue creating manga in a fun, carefree fashion.

–Rinko Ueda

Rinko Ueda is from Nara prefecture. She enjoys listening to the radio, drama CDs, and Rakugo comedy performances. Her works include *Ryo*, a series based on the legend of Gojo Bridge, *Home*, a story about love crossing national boundaries, and *Tail of the Moon (Tsuki no Shippo)*, a romantic ninja comedy.

TAIL OF THE MOON

Vol. 7

The Shojo Beat Manga Edition

STORY & ART BY
RINKO UEDA

Translation & Adaptation/Tetsuichiro Miyaki
Touch-up Art & Lettering/Mark McMurray
Design/Izumi Hirayama
Editor/Amy Yu

Editor in Chief, Books/Alvin Lu
Editor in Chief, Magazines/Marc Weidenbaum
Sr. Director of Acquisitions/Rika Inouye
VP of Sales/Gonzalo Ferreyra
Sr. VP of Marketing/Liza Coppola
Publisher/Hyoe Narita

TSUKI-NO SHIPPO © 2002 by Rinko Ueda. All rights reserved. First published in Japan in 2002 by SHUEISHA Inc., Tokyo. English translation rights in the United States of America and Canada arranged by SHUEISHA Inc. The stories, characters and incidents mentioned in this publication are entirely fictional.

No portion of this book may be reproduced or transmitted in any form or by any means without written permission from the copyright holders.

Printed in Canada

Published by VIZ Media, LLC
P.O. Box 77064
San Francisco, CA 94107

Shojo Beat Manga Edition
10 9 8 7 6 5 4 3 2 1
First printing, October 2007

www.viz.com

store.viz.com

La Corda d'Oro™

by Yuki Kure

Ordinary student Kahoko couldn't be less qualified to participate in her school's music competition. But when she spots a magical fairy who grants her amazing musical talent, Kahoko finds herself in the company of some very musical—not to mention hot—guys!

Only $8.99

Shojo Beat™
MANGA from the HEART

On sale at:
www.shojobeat.com
Also available at your local bookstore and comic store.

viz media
www.viz.com

Kiniro no Corda © Yuki Kure, KOEI Co., Ltd. 2003/HAKUSENSHA, Inc.

Currently serialized in Shojo Beat *magazine – from the creator of* MeruPuri!

VAMPIRE KNIGHT™

By Matsuri Hino

Cross over to the night..

Cross Academy is attende by two groups of students: th Day Class and the Night Class Yuki Cross and Zero Kiryu ar the Guardians of the school there to protect the Day Clas from the Academy's dark secret the Night Class is ful of vampires

Shojo Beat Manga
VAMPIRE KNIGHT
Story & Art by Matsuri Hino
1

Only $8.99

Shojo Beat™
MANGA from the HEART

On sale at:
www.shojobeat.com
Also available at your local bookstore and comic store.

Vampire Knight © Matsuri Hino 2004/HAKUSENSHA, Inc.

RATED T+ FOR OLDER TEEN

viz media
www.viz.com

NANA™

By Ai Yazawa

Nana "Hachi" Komatsu is looking for love in the big city. Nana Osaki plans to make it big in Tokyo's underground punk scene. This is the story of two 20-year-old women with the same name. Even though they come from completely different backgrounds, they somehow become best friends. The world of *Nana* is a world exploding with love, music, fashion, gossip and endless parties.

Only $8.99

Shojo Beat™ MANGA from the HEART

On sale at:
www.shojobeat.com
Also available at your local bookstore and comic store.

NANA © 1999 by Yazawa Manga Seisakusho/SHUEISHA Inc.

www.viz.com

Fall in Love Like a Comic
By Chitose Yagami
RENA SAKURA IS A HIGH SCHOOL STUDENT WITH A SECRET: SHE'S A PROFESSIONAL MANGAKA. AND ALTHOUGH SHE'S NEVER BEEN ON A DATE, THAT DOESN'T STOP HER FROM DRAWING STEAMY SHOJO SCENES. BUT WHEN THE GORGEOUS TOMOYA OKITA FINDS OUT HER SECRET, SHE FINDS HERSELF ASKING HIM OUT TO GET SOME REAL-LIFE EXPERIENCE IN LOVE!
Only $8.99
Shojo Beat
MANGA from the HEART
On sale at:
www.shojobeat.com
Also available at your local bookstore and comic store.
© 2003 Chitose YAGAMI/Shogakukan Inc.
RATED T for OLDER TEEN
ratings.viz.com
viz media
www.viz.com

Tell us what you think about Shojo Beat Manga!

Our survey is now available online. Go to:

shojobeat.com/mangasurvey

Help us make our product offerings better!

viz media

Shojo Beat

MANGA from the HEART

THE REAL DRAMA BEGINS IN...

FULL MOON WO SAGASHITE © 2001 by Arina Tanemura/SHUEISHA Inc.
Fushigi Yûgi: Genbu Kaiden © 2004 Yuu WATASE/Shogakukan Inc.
Ouran Koko Host Club © Bisco Hatori 2002/HAKUSENSHA, Inc.

Love. Laugh. Live.

In addition to hundreds of pages of manga each month, ***Shojo Beat*** will bring you the latest in Japanese fashion, music, art, and culture—plus shopping, how-tos, industry updates, interviews, and much more

DON'T YOU WANT TO HAVE THIS MUCH FUN?

Only $34.99 for 12 GIANT Issues! 51% OFF the Cover Price!

Shojo Beat
MANGA from the HEART
www.shojobeat.com
July 2005
STRAIGHT FROM TOKYO:
WIN a Mini Cooper!
PAGE 344
INTRODUCING Godchild Absolute
www.shojobeat.com

NANA
by Ai YAZAWA

Subscribe Now! Fill out the coupon on the other side

Or go to: www.shojobeat.com

Or call toll-free 800-541-7876

by MITSUBA TAKANASHI | by KANOKO SAKURAKOJI | by MATSURI HINO | by MARIMO RAGAWA | by YUU WATASE

Absolute Boyfriend © 2003 Yuu WATASE/Shogakukan Inc. Akachan to Boku © Marimo Ragawa 1991/HAKUSENSHA, Inc. CRIMSON HERO © 2002 by Mitsuba Takanashi/SHUEISHA
Backstage Prince © 2004 Kanoko SAKURAKOUJI/Shogakukan Inc. NANA © 1999 by Yazawa Manga Seisakusho/SHUEISHA Inc. Vampire Knight © Matsuri Hino 2004/HAKUSENSHA

Save OVER 50% OFF the cover price!

Shojo Beat™
MANGA from the HEART

Six of the most addictive Shojo Manga from Japan: *Nana, Baby & Me, Absolute Boyfriend* (by superstar creator Yuu Watase!!), and more! Plus the latest on what's happening in Japanese fashion, music, and culture!

Save 51% OFF the cover price PLUS enjoy all the benefits of the Sub Club with your paid subscription—your issues delivered first, exclusive access to ShojoBeat.com, and gifts mailed with some issues.

only $34.99 for 12 HUGE issues!

☑ **YES!** Please enter my 1-year subscription (12 GIANT issues) to *Shojo Beat* at the special subscription rate of only $34.99 and sign me up for the Sub Club.

NAME

ADDRESS

CITY STATE ZIP

E-MAIL ADDRESS P6BGNC

☐ MY CHECK, PAYABLE TO SHOJO BEAT, IS ENCLOSED

CREDIT CARD: ☐ VISA ☐ MASTERCARD

RATED T+ FOR OLDER TEEN

ACCOUNT # EXP. DATE

SIGNATURE

☐ BILL ME LATER PLEASE

CLIP AND MAIL TO

SHOJO BEAT
Subscriptions Service Dept.
P.O. Box 438
Mount Morris, IL 61054-0438

Canada add $12 US. No foreign orders. Allow 6-8 weeks for delivery.